MICROLIFE

A World of Micro-organisms

Revised and Updated

Robert Snedden

Heinemann
LIBRARY

www.heinemann.co.uk/library
Visit our website to find out more information about Heinemann Library books.

To order:
☎ Phone ++44 (0) 1865 888112
Send a fax to 44 (0) 1865 314091
📄 Visit the Heinemann Bookshop at www.heinemann.co.uk/library to browse our
💻 catalogue and order online.

First published in Great Britain by Heinemann Library, Halley Court, Jordan Hill, Oxford OX2 8EJ, part of Harcourt Education. Heinemann is a registered trademark of Harcourt Education Ltd.

Editorial: Clare Lewis
Design: Joanna Hinton-Malivoire
Picture research: Ruth Blair
Production: Sevy Ribierre

Originated by Chroma Graphics (Overseas) Pte. Ltd
Printed and bound in China by Leo Paper Group
10-digit ISBN 0431093474
13-digit ISBN 978-0-431-09347-5
10 09 08 07
11 10 9 8 7 6 5 4 3 2 1

British Library Cataloguing in Publication Data
Snedden, Robert
A World of Micro-organisms. – 2nd edition
– (Microlife)
1. Bacteria – Juvenile literature 2. Viruses –
Juvenile literature
I. Title
616'.014
A full catalogue record for this book is available from the British Library.

Acknowledgements
The publishers would like to thank the following for permission to reproduce photographs:
Image Select: p40; Planet Earth Pictures: p43; Science Photo Library: Dr T Brain p4 (bottom), Biophoto Associates p37, BSIP VEM pp18, 22, 31, Science Photo Library/Astrid and Hanns-Frieder Michler p5, Science Photo Library/Michael Abbey p7, M Chillmaid p13, CNEVA/Eurelios p17, CNRI pp4 (top), 12, 18, 25, A Crump/WHO p35, A Dowsett p21, Eye of Science p34, V Fleming pp15, 41, E Grave pp23, 33, J Howard p16, R Knauft p45, Dr K MacDonald p27, Prof. L Montagnier, Institut Pasteur/CNRI p10, Dr G Murti p6, Corbis p29, K Porter p9, J Reader p20, S Stammers p39, Dr L Stannard, UCT pp14, 24, A Syred p42, S Terrey p28, Dr M Wurtz, Biozentrum, University of Basel p11.

Cover photograph: The amoeboid protozoa that causes amoebic dysentery. Reproduced with permission of Corbis/Mediscan.

The Publishers would like to thank Dr Puran Ganeri and Anna Claybourne for their comments in the preparation of this title.

Every effort has been made to contact copyright holders of any material reproduced in this book. Any omissions will be rectified in subsequent printings if notice is given to the publishers.

Any words appearing in the text in bold, **like this**, are explained in the Glossary.

Contents

Introduction

There is more to the living world than simply plants and animals. We share our world with a vast number of tiny living things, many of which can only be seen with the aid of powerful microscopes. Although minute, these **micro-organisms** have a profound effect on our lives. Many can invade our bodies and those of other animals and plants, causing illness and disease. Others work quietly and unseen, breaking down animal wastes and the remains of dead plants and animals.

Viruses

Viruses are the smallest of these micro-organisms. They are so tiny and so simply constructed in comparison to the living world we know, that they exist in a shadowy borderland on the edge of life. Outside a living **cell**, a virus is very like a non-living crystal. Perhaps we should not call them organisms at all. A virus only comes to "life" when it invades a living cell and takes it over, directing the cell to make new viruses. Some viruses attack the cells of large creatures such as humans, while others attack other micro-organisms such as **bacteria**.

A single influenza virus, shown here magnified nearly 400,000 times. In some ways, viruses are classed as living things, but in other ways they are not.

Prions

Prions are even smaller than viruses, but they are not alive at all, so do not count as true micro-organisms. They are tiny molecules that live in the brain. They can sometimes act like micro-organisms and spread brain diseases.

A syringe needle used for giving injections. The rod-like shapes clustered around the tip are bacteria.

Bacteria

Bacteria are the most ancient of the truly living inhabitants of our planet. Unlike viruses they do not need to take over other cells in order to reproduce. They are capable of reproducing themselves by making use of materials in their environment.

Bacteria are found everywhere – in the air and soil, in our food and drink, and inside plants and animals. Scientists once thought they were tiny animals but later classified them as plants. Today bacteria are seen as neither animals nor plants, but as a unique kingdom of the living world.

Protists

There are over 100,000 different species of **protist**, and they live anywhere there is water. They move in their billions through water everywhere, from rain-water puddles to oceans. Some move in the moisture on grains of soil, while others live in and on animals and plants. Most protists can be seen only under a microscope, although some larger ones can grow up to 6 to 12 millimetres long. Protists can be long and thin, spiralled, or round and ball-like. Each protist consists of just a single cell, the smallest unit of life. Like bacteria, protists are neither plant nor animal, but belong to their own special kingdom of life, the Protista.

Apple-scab fungus has infected these ripe apples. This fungus damages the leaves and the fruit, ruining the crop.

Fungi

Finally there are **fungi**, the other group of life forms that is neither plant nor animal. Fungi probably makes you think of mushrooms rather than micro-organisms but some, such as yeasts and slime moulds, spend all or part of their lives as single-celled forms.

In the pages that follow we will consider these unseen kingdoms of the living world in more detail, but first we should consider exactly what it means to be alive.

What is a cell?

In biology the definition of a cell is that it is the smallest unit of life that has everything it needs for independent existence. A virus needs to make use of living cells in order to reproduce, so by this definition a virus is not itself a cell.

Some organisms, such as those described in this book, are unicellular, which means their entire body is just a single cell. The bodies of animals and plants are made up of many cells. The number of cells in a human body is around 100,000,000,000,000!

A typical plant or animal cell is around 5 to 20 micrometres (one micrometre equals a thousandth of a millimetre) in size. An average bacterium measures around 2 micrometres, with the smallest known about 0.2 micrometres.

Cell structure

A cell is enclosed by a special skin or **membrane** that separates it from its environment and from other cells. The cell membrane is one of the most important parts of a cell. It controls what passes in and out of a cell, and holds together all the other components of the cell. It allows the cell to take in substances it needs for **metabolism**, and get rid of waste substances. **Proteins** in the membrane act as "pumps", moving these substances in and out of the cell. The cell membrane is said to be "selectively permeable", meaning that some substances can get in and out but others cannot.

An animal cell greatly magnified. The nucleus (stained pink) is where the cell's genes are stored. Outside the nucleus can be seen mitochondria (stained brown), the chemical powerhouses of the cell.

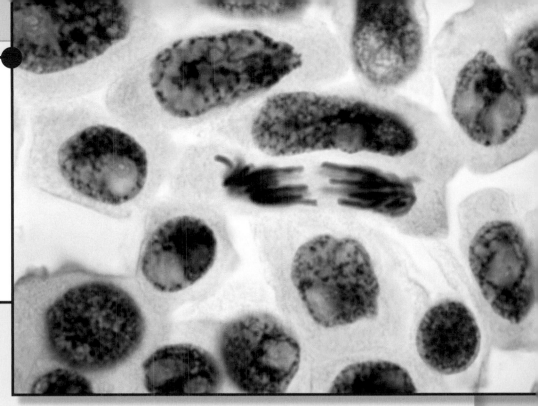

Cells dividing at the tip of a root of an onion plant. The chromosomes (the threadlike structures shown here) only become visible when a cell divides.

Some cells, including plant cells and some types of bacteria cells, have a rigid cell wall that surrounds the cell membrane and gives the cell strength and protection. Bacteria may also produce a slimy material that forms a capsule around themselves. Animal cells do not have cell walls or cell capsules.

Organelles

Around 70 to 80 per cent of a cell's weight is water, in which a variety of salts and some **organic compounds** are dissolved. At one time a cell was thought to be little more than a tiny droplet of organic material called protoplasm or "the living substance". We now know that a cell has a variety of tiny structures, known as cell organelles, which means "little organs". These organelles produce hormones, **enzymes,** and other substances that carry out essential functions in the cell. The **nucleus** is usually a ball-shaped structure near the centre of the cell. It contains the **chromosomes** and the **genes** that regulate all the cell's functions.

The cell of a bacterium is smaller and has fewer cell organelles than that of a plant, animal, or protist. It has no nucleus and its equivalent of a chromosome is a thread of **DNA**, which is generally circular and attached to the cell membrane at one point.

The chemistry of life

Cells contain many small molecules, including water and many thousands of organic molecules that are used by and produced by the cell. Even when you are asleep a vast number of chemical reactions are going on in the cells of your body as this complex chemical soup of substances is arranged and rearranged, broken apart and joined together again in different ways.

Macromolecules

Cells also contain much larger molecules that are formed by joining together smaller organic building blocks. These macromolecules can be divided into four main types: carbohydrates, lipids, proteins, and **nucleic acids**, which include DNA and **RNA**. Carbohydrates such as cellulose give strength to plant cell walls or, like glycogen and starch, are used as food stores. Lipids, commonly known as fats or oils, can be used as food stores and also form part of the cell membrane.

By far the most complex and most important of the macromolecules are the proteins. There are many thousands of proteins and each has a unique structure and task to perform. An average bacterium will have more than 2,000 different proteins. Special types of protein, called **enzymes**, control the rate of the thousands of different chemical reactions that are constantly going on inside living cells. Each reaction has its own specific enzyme. Because the enzymes control the reactions, they control the cell and the functioning of the whole organism.

Nucleic acids

The nucleic acids, DNA and RNA, are involved in the storage and transfer of genetic information. A nucleic acid consists of a long series of smaller units called **nucleotides**. There are four different nucleotides and they can appear in any order in the DNA. Each living thing has a unique order of nucleotides making up its DNA, and this provides the information needed to make each individual organism.

All proteins are made of chains of smaller molecules called **amino acids**. The instructions for making a protein are contained in the cell's DNA. A series of three nucleotides is called a codon, the code for one amino acid. Part of the cell reads off the DNA code and assembles the amino acids into proteins. The complete length of DNA necessary to code for a protein is called a gene.

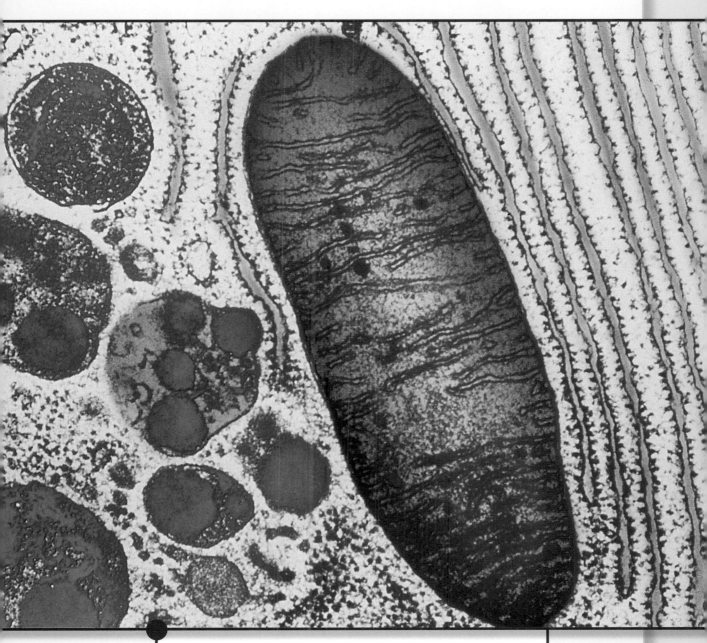

A mitochondrion inside a cell. Mitochondria are where respiration takes place, combining oxygen with sugar to provide energy for the cell.

What is a virus?

A virus is a tiny bit of matter that cannot be said to be definitely living or definitely non-living. Viruses are so small that no one had ever seen one until the electron microscope, a powerful tool capable of magnifying objects millions of times, was developed in the 1930s.

Viruses seem to be alive only when they attack living cells. When they do so, they can cause diseases in plants and animals. Polio, the common cold, chicken pox, smallpox, measles, mumps, and rabies are all diseases that are caused by virus infections. So, too, is the deadly, and as yet incurable, AIDS (acquired immune deficiency syndrome) caused by the human immunodeficiency virus, HIV.

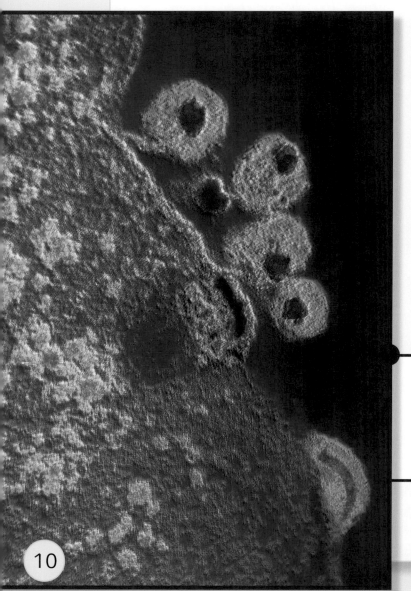

The virion

A single, infective virus particle is often called a virion. The virion has an inner core of genetic material that usually consists of a single molecule of either DNA or RNA, never a mixture of the two. A typical virus will contain about a dozen genes though larger viruses may have around 200 genes.

Human immunodeficiency viruses (HIV), which cause AIDS, seen here emerging from the surface of a white blood cell.

The capsid

The central core of a virus is surrounded by an outer protein coat, called a **capsid**. The capsid-coat of a virus has a distinctive geometric shape that is characteristic of each type of virus. **Helical** virions, such as the tobacco mosaic virus, are usually long and cylindrical. **Icosahedral** virions, such as the polio virus, have capsids that have 20 triangular sides, or faces, and are roughly spherical in shape. Some **bacteriophages** (viruses that attack bacteria) have a shape that is a mixture of the first two types. They may, for example, have an icosahedral capsid, called the head, and a long, tubular appendage, called the tail, with which they attach themselves to the surface of the bacterium being attacked.

The envelope

Some virions may acquire a membrane-like coat, called the envelope, around the capsid. This outermost coat is taken from the membranes of the cell that the virion invades. Virions that do not have an outer envelope are said to be naked.

Infection

Viruses will only invade certain cells in particular animals or plants. The common cold, for example, is caused by viruses that attack the nose and throat of human beings, but which have no effect on cats and dogs. In order to infect a living cell, a virus must first get its genetic material into the cell. Once inside the cell's defences the virus takes over and begins to produce new virus particles. The new viruses leave the cell and infect other cells. Some viruses destroy cells completely when they leave them.

A virus that attacks sugar-beet plants. The virus's genetic material is protected inside a protein casing shaped like a tube.

The "life" of a virus

Viruses live as **parasites** inside other organisms – plants, animals, fungi, protists, and bacteria. A parasite is something that takes **nutrients** or other benefits from another organism, called its host, but gives nothing in return. A virus lacks the "machinery" necessary to make nucleic acids and proteins, so in order to reproduce itself it must take over the machinery of another organism.

Hosts and reservoirs

No parasite can afford to harm its host by taking too much. If all its hosts die, then the parasite – deprived of the resources it needs – will die too. It is also a problem for the virus if the host mounts an effective resistance to the virus and becomes **immune** to it.

Many viruses that are fatal in one species may invade but have little effect on another species. For example, rabies is fatal to dogs, humans, and many other animals but it does not harm bats, in which it is also found. The bats are said to be a reservoir for the rabies virus, spreading it to other organisms but remaining immune themselves.

A rabies virus. The virus is surrounded by a membrane envelope taken from the membrane of the cell it emerged from. Without treatment rabies is almost always fatal in humans.

Jumping species

Viruses may move from one species to another and cause harm. Scientists think that the human immunodeficiency virus (HIV), the virus that causes acquired immune deficiency syndrome (AIDS), was originally found in chimpanzees. In 1999, Dr Beatrice H. Hahn and her colleagues at the University of Alabama announced their finding that the virus must have passed from chimps to humans in West Africa in about 1950. In 2006, an international research team revealed that they had found a virus very closely related to HIV in chimps in Cameroon, West Africa. They believed that it had jumped to humans in the early 20th century. No one is sure how the virus jumped, but it could have happened when hunters became injured while hunting chimpanzees, and became infected with chimpanzee blood.

Evolving together

If a virus moves from one group of animals to another it may at first be highly infectious and often fatal. Later it may become less harmful as the new host develops some defence against it. In 1950 the myxomatosis virus was found in the native rabbits of South America but was generally harmless to them. However, when it was brought into contact with rabbits that had been introduced to Australia from Europe, 99.5 per cent of the rabbits infected by the virus died. Within a few years the death rates decreased considerably, falling to below 50 per cent in some areas. This was due both to the virus **mutating** into a less destructive form that did not kill all its hosts and to the increased resistance of the rabbits to the virus. Both these changes were brought about by natural selection.

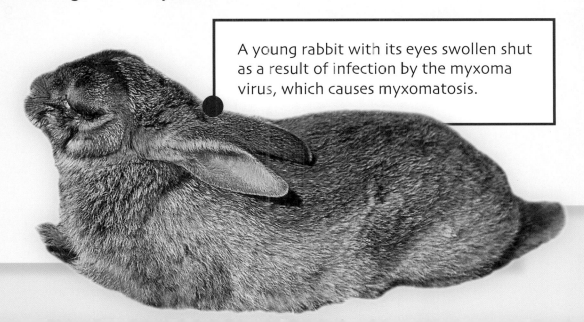

A young rabbit with its eyes swollen shut as a result of infection by the myxoma virus, which causes myxomatosis.

13

Virus attack

Viruses have different ways of gaining entry into the cells they attack. Those that attack plants find their way in through breaks in the rigid walls that surround and protect the interior of the plant cell. Sap-sucking insects may often carry a virus into a plant. Viruses that attack animal cells depend on the shape of their outer protein coat. They can fit it into the surface of the cell like a key into a lock, and then slip inside. Bacteriophages cling to the surface of a bacterium, releasing an enzyme from their tails that digests a hole in the bacterium's surface. Through this, they inject their genetic material into the cell.

Pulling the trigger

Once inside a cell, a virus may remain **dormant** for months or even years, having no visible effect on its host. Then the parts of the host cell that make proteins suddenly start to read the instructions on the virus's genetic material instead of the cell's own. Scientists do not yet understand why this happens. The biological machinery of the cell begins to make new viral genetic material and new viral protein instead of its own.

Bacteriophages – viruses that attack bacteria. The large "head" contains the virus DNA, which is injected into the bacterium through the tail.

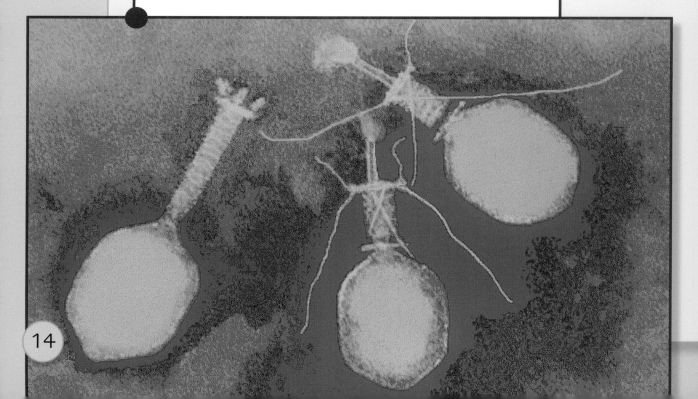

Virus assembly line

The proteins for the capsid coat and the new viral genetic material are then put together to form new viruses. Huge numbers of the new viruses can be assembled within a single cell. Sometimes, so much of the cell's machinery is taken over for virus production that it dies. The new viruses then erupt from the cell, sometimes taking some of the host cell's membrane, which forms an envelope around the new viruses. The cell may be fatally damaged, if not destroyed, by the departing viruses.

Once outside the cell, the viruses become inactive again. It is only when they are carried, perhaps in the bloodstream of an animal, in the sap of a plant, or on the wind, to another suitable cell that they will reproduce again.

Retroviruses

When some viruses invade cells their genetic material becomes part of the chromosomes of the host cell. Viruses that do this are called **retroviruses**. Whenever the host cell divides, a copy of the viral genetic material is also made. The virus may seem to have vanished, but perhaps years after it first infected the cell it can detach itself from the cell's DNA. It now begins to instruct the cell to make viral protein and DNA to make new viruses. AIDS is caused by a type of retrovirus.

Aphids feeding on a plant. As well as damaging the plant when they feed, aphids may also infect it with disease-causing viruses.

The mysterious prions

In 1982 the Nobel Prize for Medicine went to University of California biochemist Stanley B. Prusiner for his work on the proteinaceous infectious particle, or prion, the first proposed agent of infection that contained neither DNA nor RNA. The prion is a non-living protein, 100 times smaller than a virus.

The killer switch

Prions are found naturally on the surface of nerve cells in the brain. At present, no one is certain what their function might be. The prion protein usually comes in one of two shapes. One is harmless, the other is not. For some reason a prion protein sometimes takes on the harmful shape (an unknown slow-acting virus is thought by some to be the culprit). Whatever the cause or the reason for their appearance, prions can kill the nerve cells to which they are attached. Just one rogue prion can trigger the others around it to change shape. A cascade of prions fans out through the brain leaving spongy holes that will eventually cause death.

Vets examine a cow suffering from bovine spongiform encephalitis (BSE), often called mad-cow disease.

Prion-related diseases, such as kuru in humans, scrapie in sheep, and bovine spongiform encephalitis (BSE) in cows, result in an inability to walk properly, uncontrollable movements of the limbs and, in humans, distorted speech, dementia, and death, as the damage spreads through the brain.

Cannibals and cattle

Kuru existed only in a single tribe in New Guinea. It was spread by the ritual eating of human brains. Now that cannibalism has ceased there the disease is slowly dying out. Until a few years ago, the only other human disease resembling scrapie and BSE was the rare Creutzfeldt-Jakob disease (CJD), first described by two German doctors 75 years ago. The original form of CJD is now estimated to affect about one in a million people worldwide. Since 1996, however, over 100 people in the UK have died from variant CJD, or vCJD, a new form of CJD. In vCJD, the brain damage more closely resembles that found in the brains of cattle with BSE. Experts have concluded that the victims may have contracted the disease after eating meat from cattle that had BSE, although it has not yet been shown exactly how the prions can transmit the disease through being eaten.

Spreading the problem

First identified in 1986, BSE is largely confined to the UK. The source of the disease has been traced to manufactured cattle feed that incorporated the brains of scrapie-infected sheep. Following the ban on the use of **offal** in feed in 1988, the epidemic continued, which seemed to indicate that the disease could be passed on from cows to their calves. Government scientists did not admit that this was the case until 1996. It has been estimated that over 700,000 infected cattle entered the human food chain in Britain. Prions are nearly impossible to destroy and can even survive the high-temperature steam process used to sterilize surgical instruments.

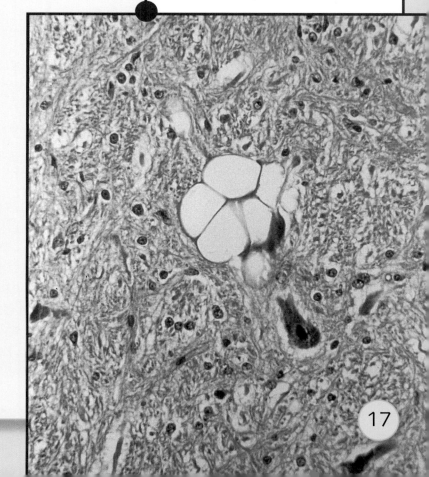

A section through the brain of a cow infected with BSE. The white spaces in the centre show where brain cells have been destroyed.

17

What is a bacterium?

A bacterium is a tiny single-celled organism. Bacteria are so small that a quarter of a million could be crammed on to the full stop at the end of this sentence. Because many bacteria have the ability to move around, scientists once thought that they were tiny animals. Then it was discovered that they had firm cell walls like plants, so they were reclassified as plants. Now it is recognized that bacteria are unique and deserve their own place in the natural world.

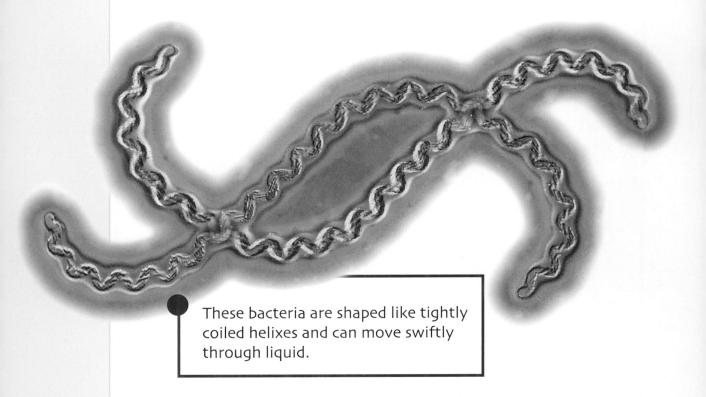

These bacteria are shaped like tightly coiled helixes and can move swiftly through liquid.

Obtaining food

Like plants, some bacteria can make their own food from inorganic, or non-living, sources. They use either the energy of the sun, like plants, or the energy of chemical reactions. Others feed on matter from other living things, just as animals do. If it were not for the bacteria that consume organisms that have died we would soon vanish beneath a deep layer of dead plants and animals. Bacteria that live in the soil break down, or decompose, dead plants and animals, making the chemical elements in their bodies available to be used by new plants as they grow.

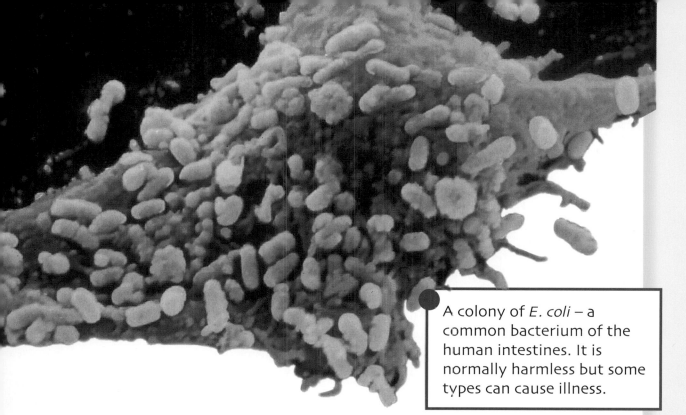

A colony of *E. coli* – a common bacterium of the human intestines. It is normally harmless but some types can cause illness.

Bacteria and disease

Many bacteria are parasites, surviving in and on living animals and plants, often causing disease. Bacteria may cause illness either by attacking the tissues directly or by producing harmful substances that cause damage.

Getting around

Many bacteria can move about by swishing tiny hair-like threads called **flagella**. These are hollow rod-like structures formed from long strands of protein that project through the bacterium's cell wall. Others have no means of propelling themselves and float aimlessly in water or on the wind, or are carried from place to place by animals they have infected.

Prokaryotes and eukaryotes

A firm layer, called the cell wall, around the outside of a bacterium encloses a jelly-like chemical soup. Unlike the cells that make up your body, a bacterium does not have a distinct nucleus containing its genetic material. Instead it has a single long strand of DNA attached to the inside of its cell membrane. Bacteria and cyanobacteria, also known as the blue-green **algae**, which lack a nucleus, are known as **prokaryotes**. All other types of cell, which have a nucleus, are called **eukaryotes**.

The oldest of all

Bacteria are the oldest forms of life we know. Tiny globules, believed to be the remains of bacteria, have been found in ancient rocks dating back more than 3,500 million years.

Stromatolites

In the shallow seas of the ancient Earth, bacteria formed thin sheets about a millimetre thick. Beneath these sheets trapped **silt** gradually built up, layer upon layer, over millennia, to form distinctive rock formations called stromatolites. If you cut into these rocks it is possible to see the fine layers. Stromatolites sometimes reached more than one metre (3 feet) in height and were common features of the early ocean shores.

Stromatolites are still being formed today in such places as Australia, the Bahamas, and the Persian Gulf. These stromatolites are, however, smaller and formed less frequently because there are now animals, such as snails, that graze on them. Billions of years ago the bacteria had the planet to themselves and had no competition. Stromatolites now tend to be formed only where grazers are kept away, for example by a high salt content in the water.

Stromatolites in the shallow water of Shark's Bay, Australia. The oldest parts are more than 2,000 million years old. The stromatolites are still forming today.

From bacteria to complex cells

Bacteria, as we have seen, differ from other cells in their lack of a nucleus, but they also lack other structures common to eukaryote cells. Prokaryotes do not have the cell organelles (little organs) called mitochondria and chloroplasts. Mitochondria are a cell's chemical powerhouses, releasing energy from sugar for the cell to use. Chloroplasts are found in green plant cells and capture the energy of sunlight to be used for **photosynthesis**. A bacterium is similar to a mitochondrion in the way it works, and in photosynthesizers, such as the cyanobacteria, the whole bacterium is similar to a chloroplast.

There is a theory, championed by the American scientist Lynn Margulis and now widely accepted, that eukaryote cells **evolved** around 1.8 billion years ago, when some bacteria acquired the ability to "capture" others, forming a symbiotic (mutually beneficial relationship) with them. A fact in favour of the theory that mitochondria are actually captured bacteria is that they have their own DNA, which is distinct from that found in the cell nucleus.

A cyanobacterium in the process of dividing to create two new bacteria. Cyanobacteria use the sun's energy for photosynthesis just as green plants do.

Bacterial behaviour

Bacteria, like humans and other living things, gather information about their environment. They can detect changes in the concentration of chemicals, such as oxygen, carbon dioxide, sugars, and amino acids, or changes in the acidity of their surroundings, for example. Bacteria that have the ability to move around can also sense changes in temperature. Photosynthetic bacteria can detect changes in the intensity of light. Just like other organisms, bacteria can act on what they learn about their environment.

Microcompass

Some bacteria have particles of magnetic iron ore inside their cells and can actually sense the direction of a magnetic field, including that of the Earth. They use this ability to swim along magnetic lines of force to reach the environment that suits them best.

Micromemory

There is some indication that bacteria may even have a primitive sort of memory. While they are swimming, they are constantly monitoring chemical concentrations in their environment, such as that of oxygen. By comparing the current concentration with the concentration of a moment ago the bacterium can determine whether it is increasing or decreasing and therefore whether or not it ought to continue in the same direction.

This is part of a colony of the bacterium that is mainly responsible for tooth decay. The bacteria turn carbohydrates into lactic acid by **fermentation**.

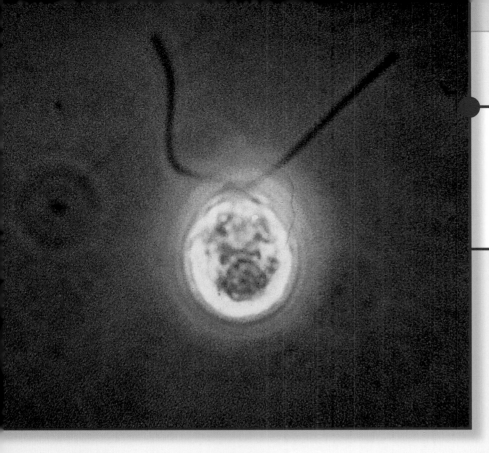

Chlamydomonas sp. is a single-celled **alga** that propels itself through the water using a pair of long **flagella**. Many bacteria also use flagella to move.

Sending signals

Some bacteria can even "talk" to each other using chemical signals. *Salmonella* bacteria, for example, release a chemical that tells other *salmonella* bacteria nearby to grow and reproduce when conditions are good.

Feeding

Bacteria can be divided into autotrophs (self-feeders) and heterotrophs (other-feeders). Autotrophs can make make their own food from non-living sources, such as sunlight or minerals. Heterotrophs feed on other living or dead creatures.

Bacteria that obtain their energy through photosynthesis are called phototrophs. The cyanobacteria use light energy in a process very similar to that in green plants, splitting water to combine hydrogen with carbon and giving off oxygen. Green sulphur bacteria and purple sulphur bacteria, on the other hand, use light energy to split hydrogen sulphide but do not produce oxygen. Some bacteria can obtain the energy they need from chemical reactions. These have the wonderfully tongue-twisting name of chemolithoautotrophs.

Bacteria and reproduction

Bacteria do not have to mate to make more bacteria. If there is enough food around, each one can simply divide in two. This is called fission. When a bacterium divides, the DNA within the cell is replicated (doubled). One copy of the DNA goes to each of the new cells, which are called daughter cells, even though bacteria do not have sexes. One bacterium becomes two, these two become four, four become eight, and so on. A single bacterium could produce more bacteria than there are people in the world in less than a day.

An exchange of information

It is possible for bacterial DNA, and therefore genetic information, to be transferred between bacteria. However, these transfers of information do not involve the cells joining together. They do not take place for purposes of reproduction and there is no increase in the numbers of bacteria involved. When bacteria exchange genetic material only a small part of their total number of genes is transferred. In true sexual reproduction the offspring receives a full complement of genes from each parent.

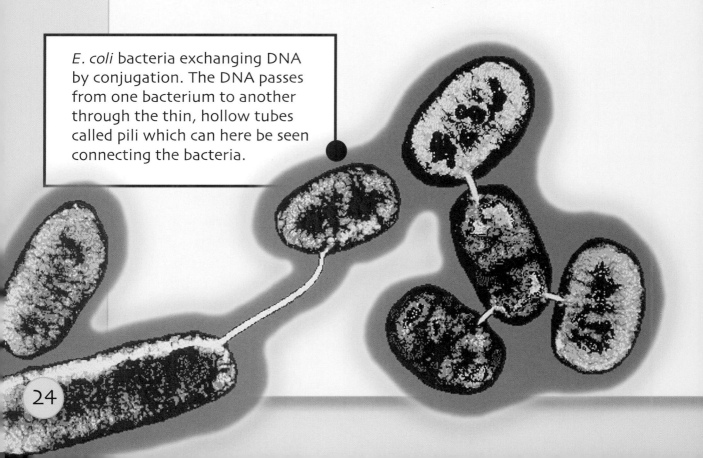

E. coli bacteria exchanging DNA by conjugation. The DNA passes from one bacterium to another through the thin, hollow tubes called pili which can here be seen connecting the bacteria.

Transformation and conjugation

There are three basic processes involved in the transfer of DNA between bacteria. One process, called transformation, involves taking up naked DNA that has come from disintegrated bacteria. This technique has been used in the laboratory to change the characteristics of a bacterium, hence the name transformation. A second process is called conjugation. This resembles mating, although strictly it is not. In conjugation the bacteria are joined by small tubular structures called pili, through which the DNA passes from one bacterium to another. Fragments of DNA can also be carried from one bacterium to another bacterium by bacteriophages, the viruses that attack bacteria. This process is called transduction.

An *E. coli* bacterium in the process of splitting to form two daughter cells. Each new cell will have a copy of the original cell's DNA.

Plasmids

Bacteria may also have very small additional chromosomes called **plasmids**. These can pass from one bacterium to another. In a phenomenon known as infectious drug resistance, plasmids can carry genes giving resistance to **antibiotics** from one species of bacterium to another. This gives whole populations of bacteria the ability to acquire resistance to drugs very rapidly.

Archaebacteria

Until 1977 it was believed that life could be split neatly into two – prokaryotes, the bacteria, which have no nucleus in their cells, and the eukaryotes, or everything else, which do.

Carl R. Woese of the University of Illinois compared molecules of RNA in different cells. RNA is one of the nucleic acids and is responsible for putting together proteins in the cell. He concluded that a group of **microbes** that had been classified as bacteria were sufficiently different on the biochemical level to be given their very own kingdom in the living world. This led to the old kingdom of the bacteria being split into two distinct parts: the **archaebacteria** (ancient bacteria) and the eubacteria (true bacteria).

The archaeans

The archaebacteria, also known as archaeans, are similar to the eubacteria in many ways. Both types of bacteria lack a nucleus for instance. The genes of the archaebacteria would seem to suggest that they are the most ancient of the Earth's life forms. They have genes that are similar to those found in eubacteria, but they also possess some genes that are found only in eukaryotes, and a large number of genes that are unique. More than 50 per cent of the genes of archaeans are completely different from any genes yet found in the other prokaryotes or in eukaryotes. Scientists are eager to learn the nature of the archaeans' unique genes and hope that they may offer valuable clues to the origin and evolution of life on Earth.

Tough creatures

Many archaeans and some eubacteria are adapted to the conditions widely believed to have existed on the early Earth, such as high temperatures and little or no oxygen. All of the archaebacteria are anaerobic (live without oxygen). Most are tough creatures found in some of the Earth's most extreme environments, near undersea volcanic vents or in salt concentrations that would kill other organisms. For this reason they are also known as extremophiles.

A black smoker vent on the ocean floor. Extremophile bacteria get their energy from the sulphur that pours from the vent.

A common ancestor?

Most scientists suspect that archaebacteria and eubacteria diverged from a common ancestor relatively soon after life began. Archaebacteria are thought to be closer to the common ancestor of both the prokaryotes and eukaryotes than are the eubacteria.

Extremophiles – life at the edge

Bacteria are as diverse and sophisticated as any other kingdom in the natural world. One bacterium can be as distinct from another as a kangaroo is from a shark. Some of the most extraordinary bacteria have been named extremophiles, because of the extreme conditions under which they live.

Extremophiles are nearly all members of the archaebacteria or archaeans. The conditions under which they are found today mirror those of the early Earth – hot, salty, and lacking in oxygen. Some of the best known of the extremophiles are the deep-sea bacteria such as *Pyrococcus furiosus* (the Flaming Fireball) found near volcanic vents 3,000 metres (9,840 feet) down on the ocean floor. Superheated lava oozes out of these vents at temperatures of up to 400 °C (752 °F). Bacteria known as hyperthermophiles are found living near by at around, and even above, 100 °C (212 °F). Some of these bacteria will even stop growing if the temperature drops below 90 °C (194 °F)!

The blue-green colour of this hot spring pool in Yellowstone National Park, United States, is caused by huge numbers of cyanobacteria, which flourish in the hot, salty conditions.

Salted bacteria

Another group of bacteria, the halophiles, live in extremely salty environments such as salt lakes and evaporation ponds where salt collects. Some salt environments are also extremely alkaline and bacteria in such environments are adapted to both high alkalinity and high salinity. A cell suspended in a very salty solution will quickly lose water and become dehydrated because water tends to flow by osmosis from areas of low solute concentration to areas of higher concentration. Halophiles deal with this problem by producing large amounts of an internal solute or by retaining a solute extracted from outside. One archaean, known as *Halobacterium salinarum* concentrates potassium chloride in its interior.

Acid lovers

From our point of view, perhaps the grimmest of all the environments preferred by extremophiles is hot, concentrated sulphuric acid. Acidophiles, or thermoacidophilic oxidizing archaebacteria to give them their full name, are bacteria that thrive in strong sulphuric acid at 85°C (185°F). The bacteria produce the acid as they oxidize metal sulphides and release metals, while at the same time providing themselves with energy.

If there is life elsewhere in the Solar System it may well resemble the extremophiles.

On Europa, one of Jupiter's moons, there is evidence of water and volcanic activity. It is possible that these conditions enable Europa to support life, in the form of extremophile bacteria.

Mycoplasmas and nanobes

Mycoplasmas are a group of extremely small bacteria that differ from other bacteria in that they lack a cell wall. The cell is bound only by a membrane like that of a eukaryote cell. The lack of a cell wall is important medically as it results in mycoplasmas being resistant to antibiotics that work by attacking bacterial cell walls.

Mycoplasmas are among the smallest free-living and self-replicating organisms. They range in size from about 0.2 to 0.8 micrometres (a micrometre is a millionth of a metre). Mycoplasmas have only about a fifth of the DNA and genetic information found in the average bacterium. This is probably just enough to produce the minimum number of proteins needed to ensure the survival of the cell. Mycoplasmas are found widely in nature. Some live harmlessly within other organisms; others live on decaying matter. However, many are agents of disease in numerous animals and plants. Few cause infections in humans, but one that does is *Mycoplasma pneumoniae*, a common cause of respiratory infection, such as pneumonia.

Nanobes

In 1998 Phillipa Uwins and a team of geologists from the University of Queensland discovered structures deep beneath the western-Australian sea bed that could possibly be the smallest living organisms, smaller even than a mycoplasma. These "nanobes" are between 20 and 150 nanometres in diameter (a nanometre is a billionth of a metre).

The nanobes were **filament**-like structures found in a sandstone core brought up from 5 kilometres (3 miles) below the sea bed at an oil-drilling site. The researchers examined the filaments using electron microscopes, X-ray **spectroscopy**, and DNA staining. Under the microscope the structures appeared to have membranes surrounding a **cytoplasm** and nucleus. The filaments also appeared to contain DNA and seemed to grow. Uwins concluded that the structures were actually colonies of organisms.

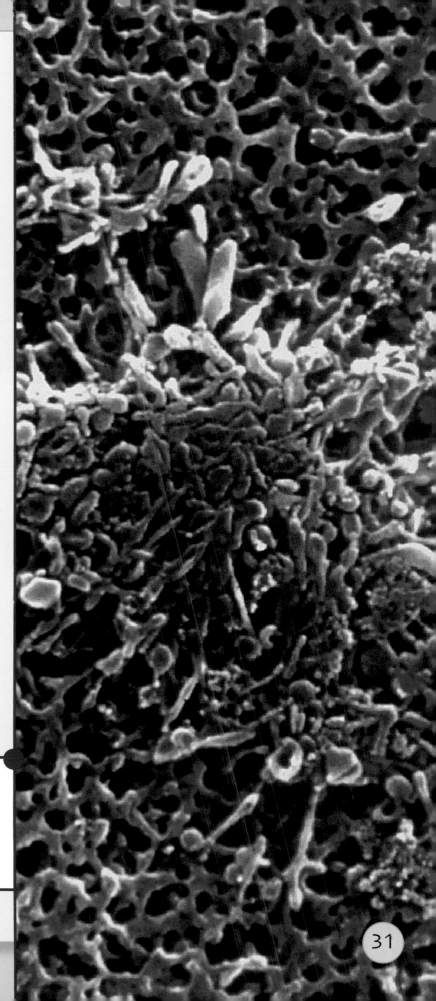

Life on Mars?

Some experts still dispute whether nanobes are really living things. However, if they are, they could support the theory that life has existed on Mars. In the 1990s, scientists found tiny worm-like shapes in a meteorite, ALH84001, thought to have come from Mars. They looked very like the nanobes discovered by Philippa Uwins, leading some scientists to suggest that they are fossilized Martian bacteria. There are plans to send unmanned missions to Mars to bring back rocks, so that the search for Martian life can continue.

Cells of the mycoplasma that is responsible for pneumonia. Mycoplasmas are the smallest single-celled life forms known.

What is a protist?

Protists are microscopic single-celled life forms that are found just about anywhere there is water. The Protista are a distinct kingdom of living organisms, alongside the bacteria, fungi, virus, plant, and animal kingdoms. Single-celled algae are also included in the Protista.

Protists are capable of carrying out all the functions necessary to sustain life, such as feeding and reproducing. Protists have at different times been classified as plants and as animals. However, they differ from plants and animals in many ways. Most obviously, each protist consists of just a single cell whereas plants and animals are made of many cells of different types. Some protists may join together in multiple-celled colonies. Most are animal-like in their need to obtain their nutrients by consuming organic matter. Some, however, can make their own food. These protists contain chlorophyll, the chemical that green plants use to capture the sun's energy in photosynthesis.

Size and structure

Protists vary in size from blood-cell parasites that may be as small as 2 micrometres in diameter, to some of the extinct water-living forms, the shells of which may be up to 10 centimetres (4 inches) in length. Colonies of radiolaria, a type of ocean-dwelling protist with hundreds of cells joined together inside a long, jelly-like sheath, can reach lengths of one metre (3 feet) or more.

Protists do not have the rigid cell wall of a bacterium or plant cell. The cell membrane that encloses a protist can change shape. Inside lies a nucleus containing the protist's genetic material, just as there is in the cells of larger, multi-celled organisms. Some types of protist may have hundreds of nuclei.

The next generation

Like bacteria, some protists reproduce by dividing into two new single-celled organisms, each with its own genetic material enclosed within a nucleus. Some protists form bud-like projections that grow into stalks to which their offspring are attached. Eventually, the next generation of protists split off.

Getting around

Protists are often divided into groups according to the way they move. One group, the flagellates, have a whip-like projection called a flagellum, which lashes rapidly back and forth to move the protist along. The ciliates have **cilia**, tiny hair-like projections that propel them through the water like the oars on a galley ship. Amoeboids creep or flow from place to place by moving the fluid around inside their bodies. Many protists cannot move by themselves but are carried along by the movements of the water in which they live.

Trichonympha protozoan lives in the intestines of termites and some types of cockroach. It moves by swishing the flagella around its body.

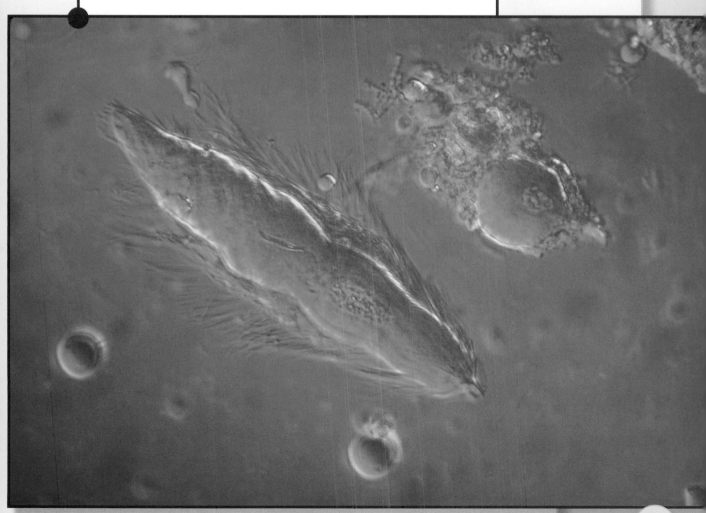

Protistan structure

The inside of a protist varies according to the particular lifestyle and habitat of the species, but some features are common to many.

All protists have one or more nuclei, containing the protist's genetic material in the form of DNA. Some species of protist have numerous nuclei inside the cell. Ciliates, for example, are characterized by having two types of nuclei, a larger macronucleus and one or more smaller micronuclei.

Vacuoles and cysts

Inside the protist there may be a clear space enclosed by a membrane. This is called a **vacuole**. There are several types and sizes of vacuole. Food is digested in some, while others store waste products that will later be ejected from the cell. Some protists have discharge devices beneath the surface membrane. These include mucocysts, which emit mucus, and trichocysts, which expel filaments. Trichocysts may be a defence mechanism.

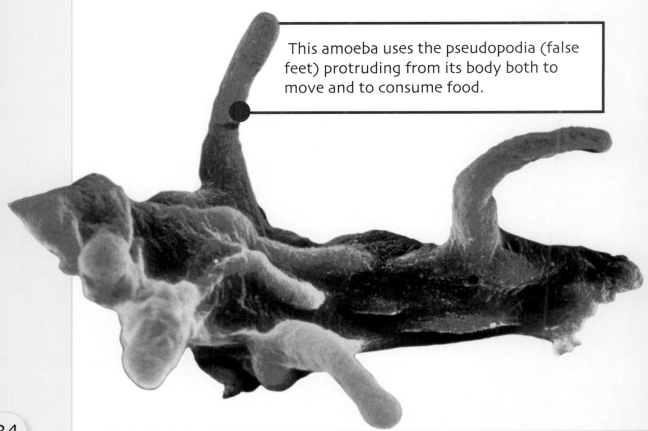

This amoeba uses the pseudopodia (false feet) protruding from its body both to move and to consume food.

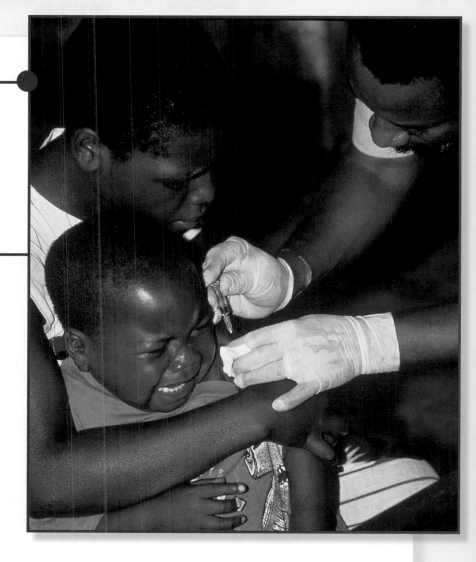

This child is being vaccinated against malaria, which is caused by a parasitic protist. The disease is becoming increasingly resistant to drugs.

Flagella and cilia

Like some bacteria, some protists have flagella, but these are quite different in structure from the bacterial version. An elaborate system of internal tubules runs the length of a protist's flagellum, making it a more complex arrangement than the simple protein filament flagellum of a bacterium. Protists can also have cilia, which are much shorter than flagella but are otherwise similar in structure and function. The patterns formed by the cilia can be used to identify various protistan groups.

Protists have a variety of coverings. Some species have an internal skeleton, others are enclosed within elaborate shells. These hard parts protect and support the soft, living material within. Radiolarian amoebae form particularly complex and beautiful skeletons with long, thin projections of living material, called pseudopods (false feet), projecting through the shell.

Protistan life

The life cycles of protists are extremely varied and can be remarkably complicated.

Some species of protist are asexual (they simply divide to produce two or more "daughter" cells in the same way that bacteria do). Other species require the fusion (bringing together) of two reproductive cells, just as sperm and an egg have to be fused in humans.

Alternating generations

Some protists are both asexual and sexual at different times in their life cycles. Some foraminifera, a mostly marine-dwelling type of protist, have alternating sexual and asexual generations, which can look quite different from each other, during each reproductive cycle. Sexual reproduction can take place, either through the release of the sex cells into the surrounding water where they fuse, or by conjugation when two parent cells exchange sex cells directly.

Finding food

Some protists are able to make their own food by photosynthesis. They have complicated structures called plastids, which contain light-absorbing pigments such as chlorophyll. Plastids can occur in varying shapes and numbers in protists. Some absorb their food directly through the cell membrane, taking in nutrients dissolved in the water around them. Most engulf tiny particles of living matter. Others hunt and capture their food, which might be bacteria or other protists. Some use both methods – photosynthesis and capturing food.

Algae associations

Some protists form associations with algae, enclosing them within a vacuole. The alga can make food by photosynthesis and some of this goes to the protist. In return the alga gets some protection inside the protist.

Solid waste is excreted by expelling it from the cell. A storage vacuole fuses with the outer cell membrane and releases the waste products into the surrounding environment. Sometimes this is done through a specialized opening on the cell's surface. Excess water and some dissolved waste products are pumped out of the cell through pulsing expulsion vacuoles.

Hard times

Many protists can survive long periods without food or suitable living conditions by forming an impermeable **cyst** around themselves. They will remain dormant inside the cyst until conditions improve.

Some protists are anaerobic, living where oxygen is scarce or absent; others require oxygen to survive. Some anaerobic protists will die if exposed to oxygen.

Didinium on the left, a ciliate protist, is caught in the act of attacking a *Paramecium*, another ciliate protist. The smaller *Didinium* will expand enormously to consume its prey.

Living with protists

Most protists play a very beneficial and important role in the environment. The plant-like photosynthesizing protists are what an ecologist would call primary producers, producing food from non-living materials. They prop up the food chain, converting atmospheric carbon dioxide into energy-containing compounds for their own nutrition. By doing so they provide a supply of nourishment for the non-photosynthesizing protists that consume them as food and these, in turn, provide a major source of food for larger organisms. This forms a chain that can stretch, via fish for example, all the way to humans.

Protistan passengers

Some animals, such as sheep and cows, would be unable to digest the grass they eat without some help from the protists that live in their guts. Ciliates, a type of protist that lives in the stomachs of grazing animals, are largely responsible for the digestion of the tough cellulose contained in the grass these animals eat. Protists are also abundant in the guts of termites, helping them to digest the wood they consume.

Toxic blooms

Some photosynthetic protists, such as certain species of reddish-coloured marine protist called dinoflagellates, can increase massively in number when conditions are favourable for their growth. This produces red tides, or toxic blooms, when huge numbers of protists stain the water red. Toxins (poisons) produced by the dinoflagellates can kill fish in great numbers. Humans, too, may become ill if they eat fish that have been contaminated by the toxins.

Parasitic protists

Very few protists are harmful to humans or their domestic animals. However, the parasitic protists are among the most serious disease-causing organisms of animals and humans, especially in tropical climates. The diseases they cause are widespread and difficult to cure. They include the malaria trypanosome, a protist that mainly invades human red blood cells during one phase of its life cycle. Malaria causes the sufferer to feel severe fevers and chills and can often result in death.

One of the dinoflagellates that are found in large numbers in the sea. Huge increases in the numbers of dinoflagellates can result in toxic blooms, which can kill large numbers of fish.

What is a fungus?

Some fungi, such as mushrooms and toadstools, can resemble plants but all fungi lack chlorophyll (the green pigment of plants that captures the energy of the sun in photosynthesis); fungi do not have stems, roots, or leaves either. These distinctive characteristics place them in their own kingdom, the Fungi.

There may be over 1.5 million species of fungi in the world. They are a large and widely distributed group living in a wide range of habitats. As well as the more visible mushrooms, they also include yeasts (well-known for their part in breadmaking and alcohol production), the microfungi or moulds that are responsible for breaking down decaying vegetation, various mildews, and the plant-disease-causing smuts and rusts. There are also the remarkable slime moulds, which have an amoeba-like feeding stage (see page 44) and which some scientists think are probably better placed in the kingdom Protista.

Parasites and saprophytes

Because fungi lack chlorophyll, , they are unable to make their own food from carbon dioxide, minerals, and water as plants can. Like animals, fungi must obtain the food they need by consuming other living, or once-living things. Fungi live either as parasites of living organisms (which can include other fungi) or as saprophytes, obtaining their nutrients from dead organisms or substances that contain organic matter.

The mushrooms we see on the forest floor are the spore-producing parts of the fungus.

The mycelium

The vast majority of fungi have a common unique characteristic, the **mycelium** or filamentous feeding system. Mycelia are composed of thread-like filaments called **hyphae**. Each individual hypha is surrounded by a fairly rigid wall made up of chitin or cellulose or both, along with other starch-like carbohydrates. The hyphae absorb nutrients and produce spores on specialized reproductive structures called sporophores or fruiting bodies. The familiar mushroom is actually a sporophore. The yeasts and the slime moulds are exceptions. Yeasts are usually single-celled organisms and do not produce true hyphae, and the slime moulds' amoeba-like stage sets them apart from all other fungi.

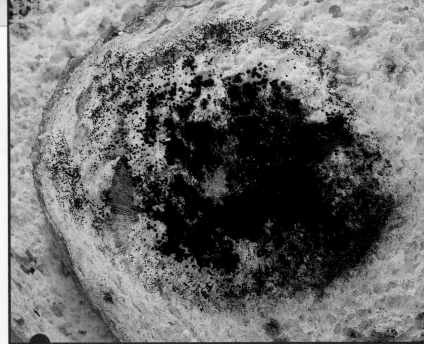

Mould growing on bread. A microscopic network of hyphae draw nutrients from the bread. What we see are the spore-producing fruiting bodies.

Spores

A spore performs the same function as a seed, but, unlike a seed, it does not contain an embryo and is usually only a single cell.

Fungal partnerships

Fungi play a vital role as decomposers in the natural world. Without fungi the breakdown and recycling of important plant compounds such as cellulose and lignin would not take place. Fungi form partnerships with plants in an association called a mycorrhiza. This is when the fungus becomes entwined with plant roots, helping the plant to take up nutrients from the soil. In turn, sugars produced by the plant pass into the fungus.

Types of fungi

Fungi are classified according to the type of spore produced and on the form of the spore-bearing structures. There is no universal agreement on this, and various classifications divide the fungi in different ways. Broadly speaking, fungi are divided into the following major groups.

Mastigomycotines

The mastigomycotines are mainly aquatic fungi with self-propelling spores called zoospores, which move using whip-like flagella. These fungi include parasites of fish and their eggs and some species that are the cause of destructive plant diseases. One species was responsible for the potato famine that devastated Ireland between 1845 and 1847.

Zygomycotines

The zygomycotines are land-living fungi that reproduce asexually by means of spores, which are sometimes violently projected into the air from sac-like structures called sporangia. In sexual reproduction two "sex-organ" structures called gametangia fuse and their contents mix, forming a thick-walled spore called a zygospore. Zygospores remain dormant for a period before they can **germinate**. These fungi are abundant in soil and dung and appear as furry growths on damp bread or rotting fruit.

A mixture of *Acetobacter* bacteria (purple) and *Schizosaccharomyces* yeast cells (beige) growing in tea. The micro-organisms are added to ferment a type of tea drunk in Russia.

Ascomycotines

The ascomycotines form the largest group of fungi. They are sometimes called sac fungi because they form spores within a sac-like cell known as an ascus.

The number of spores can vary from one to more than a thousand, depending on the species. Most ascomycotines also produce spores called conidiospores, which mean "little particles of dust". The ascomycotines are found in soil and fresh-water, and on decomposing plant and animal remains. They are important agents of both plant and animal diseases and are the cause of considerable economic loss through spoilage of foods, textiles, and a wide range of other materials.

Yeasts

The yeasts are members of the ascomycotines. *Saccharomyces cerevisiae* is used in baking and in the production of ale. Another yeast, *Candida albicans*, causes a group of diseases, including thrush. Other ascomycotines include mildews, which affect plants, and the penicilliums, used to produce the antibiotic penicillin and in the production of some cheeses. One particular group provides the fungal partner in the majority of lichens. These algal-fungal partnerships are important colonizers of new land.

A giant puffball – one of the edible fungi.

Basidiomycotines

The basidiomycotines include many fungi whose large, fleshy, fruiting bodies are generally called mushrooms, for example bracket fungi and puffballs. Most play a vital role in the decomposition of leaf litter, wood, and dung. A number of mushrooms are good to eat, but there are also a number of highly poisonous species. This group also includes the rusts and smuts, both of which cause plant diseases.

Slime moulds

Slime moulds, or myxomycetes, are a special division of the fungi kingdom. They are single-celled organisms that spend part of their lives consuming rotting wood and hunting down and digesting bacteria that live in soil. Many scientists would argue that these organisms should be classified as protists.

Detecting and signalling

A slime mould can tell how many bacteria there are around by detecting the molecules they release. It is thought that by measuring the levels of these bacterial molecules and the molecules released by other slime moulds, it can decide when the food supply is running short. A few scattered slime mould cells begin giving off pulses of a signalling molecule, called cAMP (cyclic AMP, or adenosine 3',5'-cyclic monophosphate). When nearby cells pick up the signal, they move towards the source. They send out cAMP, which attracts other cells further away. The amoeba-like organisms flow towards one another, converging in a swirling mound of 100,000 or more organisms.

Many into one

The mound begins to act as if it were a single organism. Resembling a tiny slug, no bigger than a grain of sand, it begins to move. Roughly 15 per cent of the cells now begin a process that will turn them into part of the stalk, while the remaining 85 per cent prepare to turn into spores. The cells that will form the stalk rise to the top of the mound, pushing it upwards so that they form the tip of the newly formed slug shape. These cells act like a sensitive thermometer, guiding the slug towards the soil surface by heading towards heat and light. They can detect a heat source when the tip of the slug is only a thousandth of a degree warmer than its tail.

Spore formation

The cells are held together inside the slug shape by a sheath of cellulose and other proteins. After several hours, the slug shape turns into a blob.

Slime moulds that have come together to form tiny slug-like pseudoplasmodia.

The blob becomes a slender stalk on top of which is a globe, bulging with living slime moulds, each of which covers itself in a cellulose coat and becomes a dormant spore. Other parts of the slug shape turn into cups that support the ball of spores. Another part forms a disk at the bottom of the stalk, anchoring it to a grain of soil. In this form, the colony waits until a passing beetle, for example, picks up the spores and takes them to a new place. Here, they emerge from their spores and resume solitary lives.

Sex and cannibalism

Sometimes two slime mould cells will fuse together, mixing their genes. They send out cAMP signals but this time when other slime moulds arrive the mating pair swallow them up. As more and more are consumed, the cell grows and coats itself with cellulose. It becomes dormant, waiting for the right humidity and temperature to germinate. Then it divides into thousands of smaller clones, genetically identical organisms all sharing the combined genes of the original mating pair.

Glossary

alga(e) non-flowering single-celled plant, usually living in water

amino acids naturally-occurring chemicals that are used by living organisms to make proteins. Plants and some micro-organisms can make amino acids but animals must get them from their food.

antibiotic substance produced by or obtained from certain bacteria or fungi that can be used to kill or inhibit the growth of disease-causing micro-organisms

archaebacteria group of bacteria thought to be similar to the earliest forms of life on Earth

bacteriophage virus that only attacks a bacterium

bacterium (plural bacteria) any of a large group of single-celled organisms which have no organized nucleus

capsid outer protein coat of a virus

cell basic unit of life. Cells can exist as independent life forms, such as bacteria and protists, or form tissues in more complicated life forms, such as muscle cells and nerve cells in animals.

chromosome thread-like structures that become visible in the nucleus of a cell just before it divides. Chromosomes carry the genes that determine the characteristics of an organism.

cilium (plural cilia) hair-like structure used for locomotion by micro-organisms such as protists and bacteria

compound in chemistry, a substance combining two or more elements

cyst protective structure used for resting purposes by some micro-organisms

cytoplasm material, apart from the nucleus, that makes up the internal part of a eukaryote cell

DNA (deoxyribonucleic acid) the genetic material of almost all living things with the exception of some viruses. DNA consists of two long chains of nucleotides joined together in a double helix (a shape like a twisted ladder).

dormant not active

enzyme type of protein that acts as a catalyst, altering the rate of a biochemical reaction

eukaryote organism made up of a cell or cells that contain a nucleus

evolve in biology, to develop a characteristic over a period of time as a result of mutation and natural selection

ferment chemical breakdown of sugars using bacteria or yeasts. Fermentation is used in baking bread, making wine and beer, producing cheese, and in other food production.

filament fine, thread-like structure

flagellum (plural flagella) whip-like structure projecting from some single-celled organisms, which is used for locomotion

fungus (plural fungi) any of a group of spore-producing organisms such as mushrooms and moulds

gene unit of heredity. A gene is a length of DNA and a number of genes are carried on a chromosome. A gene is a set of instructions for assembling a protein from amino acids.

germination beginning of growth of a seed or spore

helical having the shape of a helix

hyphae (singular hypha) branching filaments that make up the main body of most fungi

icosahedral polyhedron that has twenty faces or sides

immune having immunity, or the ability to resist, a particular agent of disease

membrane continuous layer, made up of fat or protein molecules, enclosing a cell

metabolism collective term for all the chemical processes that occur in living organisms

microbe another name for a micro-organism

micro-organism any microscopic living thing, such as bacteria and protists

mutate to alter as a result of mutation, a change in the genes produced by a change in DNA as it is copied during cell division. Most mutations are harmful to an organism.

mycelium collection of hyphae that make up the main body of a fungus

nucleic acids DNA and RNA. DNA encodes genetic information and RNA reads this information and translates it into protein production.

nucleotide type of organic compound from which DNA and RNA are made

nucleus (plural nuclei) central part of a eukaryote cell; it encloses the cell's genetic material

nutrient any nutritious substance found in food

offal waste parts of a butchered animal, such as kidneys, heart, liver, and tongue

organic relating to or derived from living organisms. The opposite is inorganic, or non-living.

parasite one organism living on another and benefiting without giving anything in return

photosynthesis process by which green plants and some micro-organisms make carbohydrates from carbon dioxide and water using the energy of sunlight

plasmid circular strand of DNA found in bacteria that is separate from the main chromosome DNA

prokaryote cell that lacks a nucleus. All bacteria are prokaryotes.

protein one of a group of complex organic molecules that perform a variety of essential tasks in living things, including providing structure and controlling the rates of chemical reactions

protist any single-celled eukaryote that is a member of the kingdom Protista

retrovirus virus that contains RNA as its genetic material rather than DNA

RNA (ribonucleic acid) found in different forms within cells, RNA is involved in the process by which the genetic code of DNA is translated into the production of proteins in the cell

silt very fine particles of sediment, soil, and rock fragments carried by water

spectroscopy study of spectra (singular spectrum), which are electromagnetic energies arranged according to their wavelength

vacuole chamber surrounded by a membrane, found inside some types of cell.

virus infective particle, usually consisting of a molecule of nucleic acid in a protein coat

Further research

More Books to Read

Science Answers: Microlife, Anna Claybourne (Heinemann Library, 2005)

Micro World: Microscopic Life in Your Body, Brian Ward (Franklin Watts, 2006)

Microlife That Makes Us Ill, Steve Parker (Raintree, 2006)

Using the Internet

Explore the Internet to find out more about micro-organisms. You can use a search engine, such as www.google.com, and type in keywords such as *bacteria*, *viruses*, *protists*, or *fungi*. These search tips will help you find useful websites more quickly:

* Know exactly what you want to find out about first.

* Use only a few important keywords in a search, putting the most relevant words first.

* Be precise. Only use names of people, places or things.

Index

Titles in the *Microlife* series include:

Hardback   978-0-431-09344-4

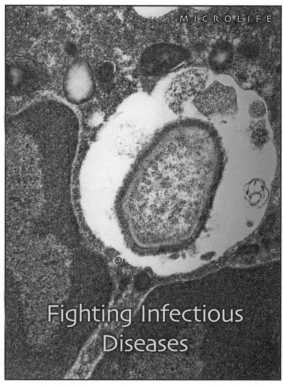

Hardback   978-0-431-09345-1

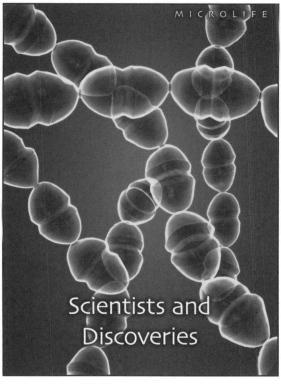

Hardback   978-0-431-09346-8

Hardback   978-0-431-09347-5

Find out about other titles from Heinemann Library on our website www.heinemann.co.uk/library